WARSCAPE
WITH LOVERS

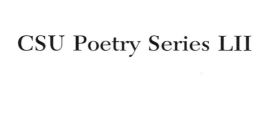

CSU Poetry Series LII

Marilyn Krysl

War–
scape
with
Lovers

Cleveland State University Poetry Center

Contents

My wife had laid our children side by side
She had placed the smallest between the other two
She had laid the boy between his two sisters
They liked to walk that way, one on either side

3. Wife

After the mine the soldiers came
Among those men they took was my husband
They made the men circle the crater three times
Then the soldiers forced them into the center

The third one herded in was my husband
Where I stood I could see his face as they shot him
I watched as one by one the others fell
Their bodies one above the other, sticks of wood

I have seven children   I know my husband's body
After the burning I did not know his body
After the burning I did not see his face again
This cloth is a piece of his sarong, partly burned

Bank: Colombo

Where the road wound down toward the sea
they cordoned off. The length that was the Green
is leveled dirt. That blackened steel's the bank.
The hotel windows, boarded up, look mean.

Only the sea still flings its cries into
the air, the way it did when we walked by.
The bomb was made abroad: someone paid cash.
People say *I couldn't even cry.*

We gave away our cash and thought this kind.
You said you loved me. How blind with need
we were, like this country. Above the sand
two wings, a single gull. The place feels numb:
no gods here. I know the feel of stone.
See that stone? Stones lie where they were flung.

1

—*The elephant, bound, thinks longingly
of the elephant grove.*
                    —The Hinayana

Look: see the peasant blasted at his crop.
The refugees kidnapped, made to carry ammunition.

The missiles dismantled, rebuilt, reinstalled.
The carcinogenic apples, the bereft gorilla mother.

The Vietnam vet propped against plate glass.
The six-year-old girl, the photographs of the body.

Friend phones long distance, love affair going badly.
I've forgotten the word for the double bladed axe.

Meanwhile the sky goes on with its watercolor.
Leaves, gorgeous, fall. The baby cries to be fed.

I feed the baby, watch the sky do its masterpiece.
The peasant again, rice green, his face burst open.

2

Flying over the heads of strangers—is this strafing?
In the museum with his father the boy admires armor.

The gorget, the lancerest, the loinguard, the breastplate
beneath which the heart pumps, the heart longs.

Look: see the seventy different kinds of daggers!
See how the headpiece stuns with its brightness!

Now think Whitman. Grandeur, think westward expansion,
the planet a sphere. Boots, guns, the fast car,

quick now, the necktie, the shot glass, the bar graph,
the radar screen, the printout of the body count—

How this energy cries out for use, satisfaction!
Bam. The young brave knocked from his pony.

Bam. The guerrilla, a spasm in foliage.
Now the woman, babe at her breast. Bam bam bam.

3

Watch my chic black. I attract the damaged man.
He sees a deep breast, a spring of milk.

He thinks if he touches me, if I let him touch me,
his hands will heal, he will play the piano again,

and his feeling, boarded up in rage,
will come forth and stand in the light, upright.

He imagines the water, its hands, their balm.
He imagines the queen in her fat honeycomb.

I take the first plane to the other side of the world.
When I arrive, he's there, waiting.

He thinks love heals, he thinks I am the healer.
He imagines the damaged can repair one another.

4

The men, the famous, fascinating men. Where are they?
And their scintillant wives, the printouts of the figures.

Are they breathing the carbon monoxide in the coke plant?
Do they work the mines, build the silicate molds?

Can they breathe? Can they work? Can they stand up?
Can they keep down food? Can they work again tomorrow?

Kick a chair, smash bottles in the street, stone cars.
Drown a cat. Hold down a girl. Hold down a girl.

Was she beautiful? Joyful? Was she mouthy? Was she handy?
Was it something to do? Was it just for the hell of it?

Would you do it again, if you could get away with it?
Have you done it again? How many times have you done it?

9

Bikini, 1953

A man came to our island. He came in a great ship.
He had many men. He said they needed our island.

He said Pack your belongings. We did not know what to do.
We did as he said. We did not know why.

The day they took us away no one ate any food.
The day they took us away no one ate any food.

When we looked back we saw the sea rise up.
Came then a great wave boiling across the water.

And the sky above the sea they darkened and burned.
They took us to an island where the water was bad.

Now we are no longer kind to each other.
I grieved for my garden, for the boat I had to leave.

In my last days there is no happiness.
In my last days I cannot go home.

10

The Palestinian boy throws rocks at the Israeli soldier.
The Israeli soldier beats up the Palestinian boy.

What is the self, this hypothetical piece of turf?
Perhaps after all it does not wear skirts.

Perhaps after all it does not wear a tie,
has no keys, no checkbook. No desire to own a mortgage.

Doesn't care which brand relieves cold symptoms sooner.
Does not desire a faster, sexier compact.

Does not wear a badge, does not carry a weapon,
does not plant flags on hillsides said to be captured.

The self is not a square, a rectangle, a pentagon.
The self is neither a circle nor a sphere.

The self exceeds the boundary of the single ego,
the genus, the family, the class order phylum,

includes the home court and the enemy battalion,
includes both sides and the border between them.

Includes the others: animal, vegetable. Mineral.
Includes the other colors, shapes, the other genitals.

Meanwhile here stand the frightened, and we are many.
When the earth burns, the frightened will inherit the earth.

stunned onlooker,
at outer edge
of shadow circle
cast by interloper

Death: I merely
attend, in awe,
this great work
Breath

Famine Relief

Explain, please, this wonder, this
creaturous pleasure,

this ruby of feeling
while I feed another being: tell me why

when Hasina opens her mouth,
it's as though the world in its entirety

opens, the lotus of Buddha unfolding
its jewel. Veil of skin, draped over

bone: Hasina's fourteen, so thin
she can't walk, sit up,

hold a cup. Eyes a single beam
scanning for food, even when

she's full. She's the mouth
of the soul, open

around hunger, asking
the way a baby, without guile,

is good with greediness
to know the world. To feed another being

is like eating: both of us
filling ourselves

with the certainty that there is,
in us and around us,

kindness so infinite
that we cannot be lonely. Hasina

might have been the one with the spoon,
fleshy, of substantial body,

I the skeleton—but that too would be
wrong. Under the pull of full sun

at noon, I hear the temple
gong, summoning the faithful,

and in the lull of echo,
the jangle of bells on the women's

ankles. Hasina looks up,
I lift the spoon, balancing the pans

of our scale: ours
is a life of satiety

and hunger, the haves and the have nots,
these two conditions

spread through the universe
so that we may know hunger,

so that we may learn
to feed each other. Not perfection

but the lesson, enacted over
and over again: Hasina and I

by chance or quantum design,
chosen to perform this hallowed, ancient

devotion—one the Venus of Willendorf,
each of those many breasts

overflowing, the other Kali
in her starved aspect,

shrill around emptiness,
and devouring, devouring.

Kalighat Hospice, Summer Solstice

Evening lowering, the lessening of light in its going
Leaves flickering in and out of slow dark's weave
Nuns gone up the stairs to prayer and dream
Only I am here, the last one leaving

Walking down this aisle, the women already sleeping
Shifting waves, each breath drifting into the others
And now, among the beds, a swell, sudden and rising
The girl, on her side, spine curled round her cancer

Gestalt of her body a swell in this ocean of breath
As though holding her hurt self out to the light
And flowing out from her spine a glowing fin
God energy, fanning out from the body

And if I should leave her alone, tell me
Something holds the wave together and disperses it
Something perfect, disfigured and divine
So be it, so it is   I am the one who lies down

Slides with her into the scintillant blur of electrons
Circling us the way gulls spiral over ocean
Streamers in air   Wisp lengths of airborne cloud
Strands of fine linen torn by many hands

Wrappings for the dissolving body's winding
Ash   stargas   nebulous   drifting   ghostcloth
Parachute silks, thousands, spiraling around us
Circling   ritual of wrapping   shroudcloth

While somewhere else a place is prepared
How long can we float in this ceremony of shape
How long can she anchor in my material arms
Her hand on mine, asking my skin to speak

And what shall I say *Yes, you are   and are*
Yes you are going away before us
All of us going where you go across water
Our longing going before us where we follow

There is nothing to do, nowhere to go
I lie along her length, the length of my body open
Knowing with the porous wave of my body
The wave of the one who is going away

Is it now   Now a swell's soft bloom
Pushing the water up, water going above itself
Rising in a glide, now hugely above itself
Something perfect, disfigured and divine

This is the god rising, going out, tongues burning
The water burning   the water lit with flame
Up toward the vast, unfathomable light
Down toward the vast, unfathomable dark

I am the last one to give her water—
The last to lie beside her like a lover—
The last one she touches with her long fingers—
The one here now   The one from whom she goes

And like a swell's sheer falling to the wave's floor,
Long in its slow, suspended plunge,
she falls away   The waters' huge descending
now rising, closing over her head—

See the black bark going from shore, sliding her
out of the cells: soul cargo, shimmering away—
Leaving on the surface these flecks of foam
The trillion trillion bubbles bursting

And myself, here at the circling equator
Here at the zenith of the circling year
Afloat below the nuns' high singing
Afloat on the breath of the women sleeping

Afloat on dark, on sweat, afloat on loosening strands
of light   Who am I now: single syllable
Pouring of the blood's ferocious requiem unfurled
Another wave rolled open, holding the dead girl

Transfiguration

The blind talk of a way out. I see.
—Bertolt Brecht

The last day was a day of excrement—
on the sheets, sarongs messed with it,
every other woman needing a bedpan,
then you had to empty them, rinse

and begin again. I began over.
Washing another woman my mantram.
This is the way to the worms' home.
Soon it will be your turn.

The sun sank. Late light, huge,
diminuendoed toward black. The room
stank, though it was still the cathedral.
The beds were low, you had to kneel:

I dipped a handful of rag in a bowl,
watched the water gather in its threads.
Little by little the water filled it
to the lip with the shine of wetness.

IV: LOVE

Trinity: Tea for Three

Sister Ignatius and I drink tea. Below,
the bay. The Bombay sea is gray
slate. Late afternoon, and would you say
that's a storm

brewing? Or say the sea
is brown, light slung. Shimmering lung,
it breathes great fits and starts. Ignatius
takes sugar. We are talking

of our thrilling anger, how it is like
a great love. Sister, look:
there is languor in the sea,
even when it bares

its fangs. How it bangs the shore:
importunate sea, such slippery water!
Ours the langour of slippery angels,
our anger liquor, and we are

drunk with it. (Shall I say
this tangerine is sanguine?)
Now wind winds up a storm, unfurls
the curtain. One virgin,

one whore, yes, let it pour,
to be in the world is sinful, don't
shut the window. (Sister
has married herself to Christ,

but the monsoon sea does not
give a damn. And the tea cup's lip
is the thinnest
china.) The wind is breath,

breathing us. The armure of her habit
texture in my fingers. Many
the sanguine tangerines we've eaten,
many the many we've rocked

in the dark. God
himself is dark, brilliant,
terrible. Well
rounded. We have rocked him

as well: he will not strike us
dead. Instead, what seemed a storm
splits open,
lets down a fan

of light: we watch that fan
unfurl: his hand
pulling aside the veil
to look at us here. (A cheap

shot: is that what you
thought? Is the beautiful
more than you can
handle?) Sister Ignatius and I

are lovers. Drunk on the torn
moment, its radiant
rags. We love the broken things
of this world. Kiss

the broken bodies. Here, Sister,
take this sanguine section
of tangerine, bite in: while the light
fills us. And another thing:

Christ is our consort,
and the sea's an animal
turning over in its bed.
How many hands are there

in this world! Sister,
let me whisper in the whorl
of your ear: see where Christ
swears with us the anguine

vow. I swear Christ bows
before us: the sky a shout.
The sea is many pairs of hands
holding each other, crying out.

Carpe Diem: Time Piece

In the next seat the young man from Bangalore sleeps,
or so it seems. I dream, toss, lean—
do I?—into his shoulder. Or say his shoulder
slides—does it?—against mine. A woman reads
the *Times* across the aisle, and Big Spender sun
puts money on the Pacific. My breast, that heap

of wheat Solomon sang. Bangalore's heaped
hand, my breast a hill where swallows sleep
as though they've drunk some sweet elixir. Sun
burnishes the sea, I close my eyes, lean
into his long fingers. Listen, I've read
The Song. Eyes closed, it's like that. His shoulder,

armored, gleams: a buckler's brass. My shoulder
stakes the linen tent. Now conjure heap
of my belly, thicket of hair. (Later I'll read
Mary Oliver.) Years before I'd slept
with someone blind, my body braille. We lean
into our book. The text reads us. The sun

looks sideways at the sighing sea. The sun
looks on, our hands mouths. My hand shoulders
forward, looking for antelope, a leaning
slope. Cunning hunter, crossing the heaped
savannah of his lap. Afterward, sleep
is milky sweet. I've read Duras, I've read

Huang O, Rabindranath Tagore. I've read
the Tao, and David Bohm. Each day the sun
lays down its ultimatum. Be: don't sleep
away this blazing gift, your life. His shoulder,
my eyes, his eyes: we look our fill. That heap
of sea is called a swell. It's not who leans

on whom, not gender, not power. I've always leaned
toward earth, air, water. Fire. I read
the body's scripture, freely chose. A heap

down to her knees. As sun pours
into dark, honor the damp instants. Not bathos
but glory. Water is God's womb. Know

your origins: know the amniotic, that hairy
place where the waters of Paradise pour into the earthly
compass. Sea's a woman bathing herself.

Poem for Extraordinary Day

When I've worked hard and am done, I go out from that place
and look up at the sky. It comes to me then
how substantial good work is, how it
empties and fills us, the way birds
wheel across clouds, filling and emptying and filling

the heavens. If there's grass, I lie down and look up
a long time. Then I walk home, slow like the light
going slowly
into another form

of itself. I come where you sit
in the solemnity of evening, and we watch it
get dark, taking our time, then sitting down
at the table, eating something,
noticing all the little things
about each other
we like to remember, and talking
of all that has happened
with that slow calm that comes at the end of a day

like the calm in a body of water
nothing disturbs. In that leisure
I look at you
for the pure sake of drinking in what I see,
until we move closer, touch each other
and go on touching, coming finally
to the end of what resembles,
when you're thirsty, a drink of cold

water. And when we have done these things,
I will be full, and it will time then
to flick off the light
and let everything go—
because I will have known the immeasurable pleasure
of filling a day
with the good things there are to do,